IMAGINE IF YOU HAD THE POWER OF UNPREDICTABLE TIME TRAVEL. WOULD IT BE A BLESSING OR A CURSE?
That's the question 15-year-old Nickolas Flux ponders every day of his life.
ROME
GREEK EMPIRE
19th. CENTURY
HISTORY II
POMPEII
SUMERIANS
EGYP
His first time leap surprised him during science lab.
Record the ice block's properties.
One minute he tapped a chunk of ice ...
TAP TAP!
FZZZZT!
Oh, no!
... the next he was eye to eye with a giant iceberg!

3 0036 01368 8005
For a history buff like Nick, experiencing the sinking of the *Titanic* was thrilling.
I can't believe this is happening!
Luckily, his adventure ended ...
FZZZZT!
... as quickly as it began.
I'm alive?!
Since then, Nick has discovered he has a knack for landing in history's tightest spots.
Time to practice.
AHHHHGH!
It's anyone's guess where he will end up next.
THE QUESTION IS, CAN HE SURVIVE IT?

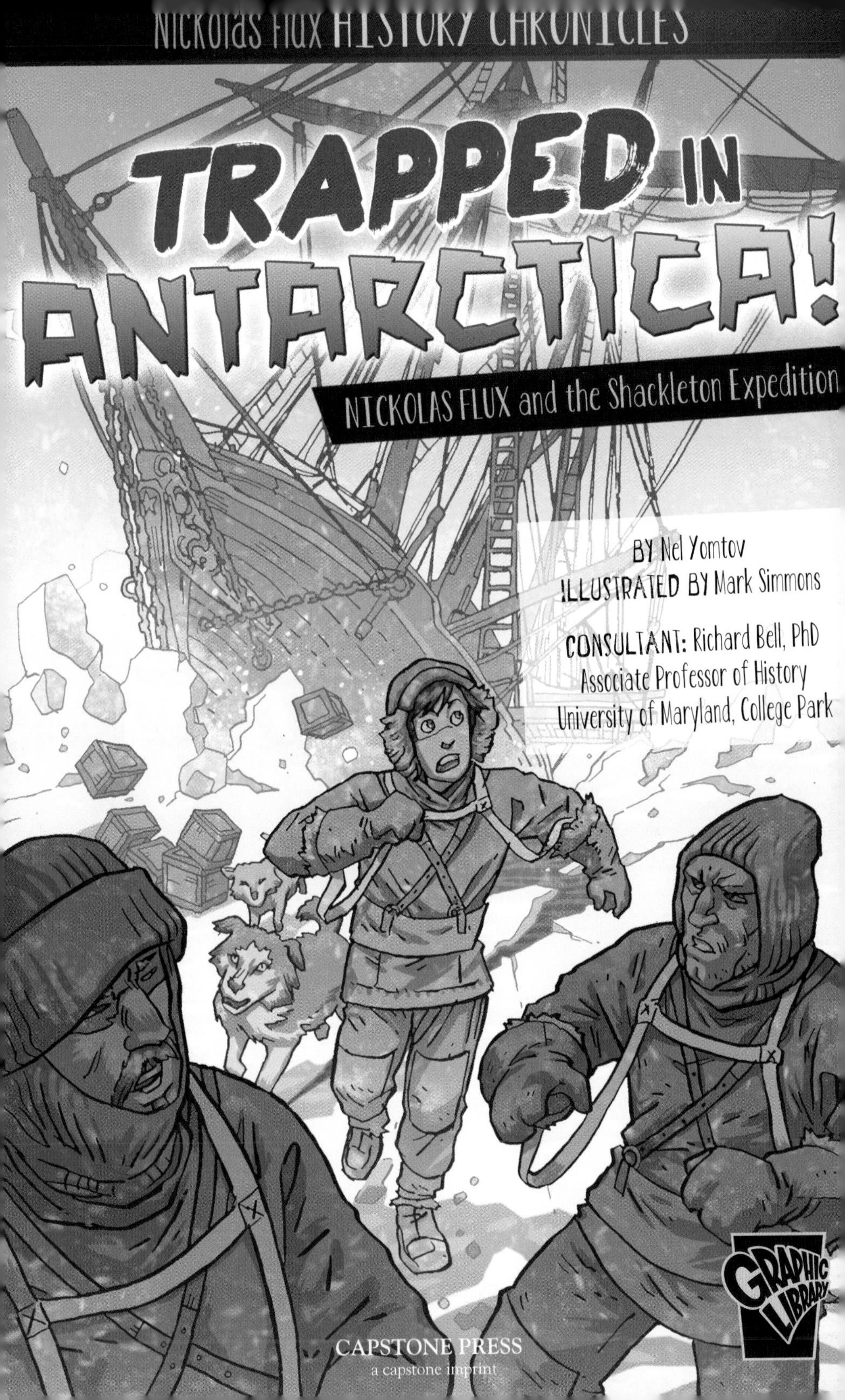

Nickolas Flux HISTORY CHRONICLES
TRAPPED IN ANTARCTICA!
NICKOLAS FLUX and the Shackleton Expedition
BY Nel Yomtov
ILLUSTRATED BY Mark Simmons
CONSULTANT: Richard Bell, PhD
Associate Professor of History
University of Maryland, College Park
GRAPHIC LIBRARY
CAPSTONE PRESS
a capstone imprint

Graphic Library is published by Capstone Press,
1710 Roe Crest Drive, North Mankato, Minnesota 56003
www.capstonepub.com

Library of Congress Cataloging-in-Publication Data
Yomtov, Nelson.
Trapped in Antarctica! : Nickolas Flux and the Shackleton expedition / Nel Yomtov.
pages cm.—(Nickolas Flux history chronicles)
Summary: "When a spontaneous time leap sends Nickolas Flux back to Ernest Shackleton's ill-fated Endurance Expedition to Antarctica, what's a teenage history buff to do? Try to avoid becoming stranded, of course! From the crushing of the Endurance to a heroic lifeboat journey, Nick must survive one of the most amazing expeditions of the early 1900s"—Provided by publisher.
Includes bibliographical references.
ISBN 978-1-4914-2069-0 (library binding)
ISBN 978-1-4914-2285-4 (paperback)
ISBN 978-1-4914-2287-8 (eBook PDF)
1. Shackleton, Ernest Henry, Sir, 1874-1922—Juvenile fiction. 2. Graphic novels. [1. Graphic novels. 2. Shackleton, Ernest Henry, Sir, 1874-1922—Fiction. 3. Imperial Trans-Antarctic Expedition (1914-1917)—Fiction. 4. Antarctica—Discovery and exploration—Fiction. 5. Endurance (Ship)—Fiction. 6. Survival—Fiction. 7. Stowaways—Fiction. 8. Time travel—Fiction.] I. Title.
PZ7.7.Y66Tr 2015
741.5'973—dc23 2014019813

Photo Credits:
Design Elements: Shutterstock (backgrounds)

Editor's note:
Direct quotations, noted in red type, appear on the following pages:
Pages 9 and 10 from *Endurance: An Epic of Polar Adventure*, by F. A. Worsley (New York: W. W. Norton, 1999).
Pages 13 and 16 from Huntford, R. "Shackleton," (New York: Carroll & Graf, 1998).
Page 17 from *The Diaries of Frank Hurley, 1912-1941*, by Frank Hurley (New York: Anthem Press, 2011).
Page 25 from *South: The Story Of Shackleton's Last Expedition, 1914-17*, by Sir Ernest Shackleton (North Pomfret, Vt.: Trafalgar Square Pub., 1992).

EDITOR
Adrian Vigliano

DESIGNER
Ashlee Suker

ART DIRECTOR
Nathan Gassman

PRODUCTION SPECIALIST
Kathy McColley

Printed in the United States of America in Stevens Point, Wisconsin.
092014 008479WZS15

TABLE OF CONTENTS

INTRODUCING ...
NICKOLAS FLUX
CAPTAIN
FRANK
WORSLEY

SIR ERNEST SHACKLETON
PERCE BLACKBORROW
THE CREW

CHAPTER ONE
THE UNEASY FISHERMAN
I'm glad the boys could join us today, Mr. Flux. Nick and Chuck look like fine fishermen!
I can't wait to get started! What will we be trying to hook, Captain Connors?
Looks like a good day for flounder, Chuck.
Seems like your brother is ready to get underway, Nick. Have you ever been out fishing?
Uh ... well, not really, Captain. I guess you could say I'm not the oceangoing type.
Ha! You can say that again. Nick gets seasick every time he's on a boat!
I do not, Chuck! Anyway, how would you know?
Easy, boys. Do me a favor, would you, Nick?

Bring those ice chests and some of our gear down below. I'll take Chuck up for a look at the steering equipment.
Do you need a hand, Nick?
No thanks, Dad. I can handle it.
Chuck's right. I'm beginning to feel a little queasy being on this boat.
Maybe I can just ignore it—
Oh no. I do feel sick. Maybe this wasn't such a good idea after all.
Ugh. Who am I kidding? I'm not a sailor.
My head is spinning and I'm getting dizzy. I feel like I'm going to—
FZZZZT!

KRRRK GRRRRK
CHAPTER TWO
TRAPPED
October 24, 1915
The hull has given way! We're taking in water!
I-I'm in the hold of an old ship that's sprung a leak! B-but are we sinking?!
Get the engine room pumps going! We can't let the engine fires be put out!
KRRRK GRRRRK
That roaring sound ... it's deafening! What could it be?!

FLUX FACT

The *Endurance* left England on August 8, 1914. Aboard the ship was leader Sir Ernest Shackleton, a crew of 26 men, 1 stowaway, 69 sled dogs, and 1 cat. Shackleton's goal was to become the first explorer to cross the continent of Antarctica on foot.

How bad is it, Captain Worsley?
Besides the deafening roar of the ice crushing in on us, water is getting into the engine rooms, Mr. Shackleton.
I see.
KRRRK GRRRRK
The crack in the hull was only 8 inches wide earlier today. Now it's grown to 2 feet.
Endurance is twisted and listing badly. The ship can't live in this, Skipper.
What the ice gets, the ice keeps.

FLUX FACT

Endurance became trapped in pack ice on January 19, 1915. For ten months it drifted with the slowly moving ice across the Weddell Sea—roughly 600 miles (966 kilometers).

CHAPTER THREE
THE ROAD TO SURVIVAL
October 27, 1915
Be careful with those supplies, boys. When you finish unloading, bring off the rest of the sled dogs.
Then I want the *James Caird* lifeboat lowered.
As for you, Nick ...

FLUX FACT

When 18-year-old stowaway Perce Blackborrow was discovered, Shackleton reportedly flew into a rage to scare the teen. "Do you know that on these expeditions we often get very hungry, and if there is a stowaway available he is the first to be eaten?" he said.

We can't stay here forever, Skipper. What's our next move?
In a few days, we'll march across the ice to Robertson Island, about 200 miles northwest.
200 miles?!
Cheer up, Nick. I need you to help prepare for the journey.
October 30
Now we start for Robertson Island, boys!
Keep at it, Nick! You're doing a fine job.
Aye, aye, Skipper!
November 1
It's useless, Skipper. We've traveled only three miles in three days. The men are exhausted and losing hope.
We'll make camp here and wait for the ice to break up.

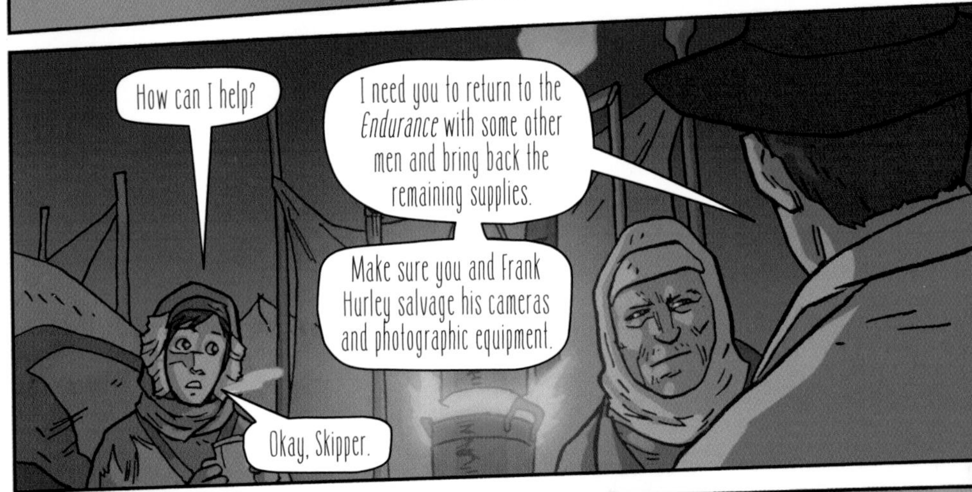

FLUX FACT

The crew established Ocean Camp on a 20-foot (6-meter) thick ice floe about 1.5 miles (2.4 kilometers) from the *Endurance*. The original camp at the *Endurance* was called Dump Camp.

November 21
She's going, boys!
It's a sickening sensation. Without *Endurance*, our isolation from the world seems more complete.
Worse, the skipper may lose the respect of his crew.
I've grown to admire that ship. Now we're alone.
I wonder what will become of us.
December 23
Weeks have passed and the ice still hasn't broken up, Skipper.
That's why we're moving out again, Nick. The men are getting restless, and I've had arguments with some of them. We've got to try to reach Paulet Island again.
We'll leave the *Stancomb Wills* here and take only two lifeboats. Maybe we'll have better luck this time with a lighter load.

FLUX FACT

In his diary, photographer Frank Hurley wrote a farewell to his favorite dog, who was ordered to be killed: "Hail to thee old leader Shakespeare, I shall ever remember thee—fearless, faithful, and diligent."

April 7
There! The mountains of Elephant Island! Just like the ones we saw earlier today on Clarence Island.
The ice pack we're on is finally crumbling. Strong ocean currents are carrying us along.
Does this mean we'll reach land soon?
Not necessarily, Nick. These currents can blow us even further out to sea. We'll just have to keep our fingers crossed.
April 8
Look! A break under the *James Caird!*
Tell the skipper, Nick! The time has finally come for us to launch the boats!
With pleasure, Captain!

FLUX FACT

The crew of the *Endurance* had spent 170 days drifting on a floe of ice with short supplies of food and inadequate shelter. Before they landed on Elephant Island, they had not set foot on land since December 5, 1914—497 days earlier!

CHAPTER FOUR
LITTLE HOPE
April 20
Many of the men are sick and in pain, Skipper. Rickinson may have suffered a heart attack. Others, like Blackborrow, have bad frostbite.
I know, Nick. This land offers little protection from the biting cold and frigid winds.
Conditions on Elephant Island are almost as bad as those on our boat journey here.
The crew is demoralized too. They haven't done any work since we got here.
We can't stay. We've got to do something.
I have an idea, Nick. Gather the men.
OK, Skipper.

FLUX FACT

Shackleton chose a small crew to accompany him to South Georgia Island including Captain Worsley, carpenter Chippy McNeish, and doctor Tim McCarthy.

April 22
Where did McNeish get the wood to fix the holes and strengthen the deck of the *James Caird*?
He took the planks from the other two lifeboats.
Next, he'll cover the top of the hull with canvas. Once we're on the rough seas, we've got to keep water from filling the boat.
Good idea. In the meantime, I'll help Captain Worsley gather the charts, maps, and supplies we're taking.
April 24
Wish us luck, boys, and keep your spirits up! We'll be back with a rescue party soon enough.
I'm worried about the men we're leaving behind. Without proper clothing and shelter, they might freeze to death.
And if we fail to reach help, they'll have no chance at all to survive.

FLUX FACT

Captain Worsley used a sextant to navigate the *James Caird*. This instrument measures the angle between the Sun, moon, or a star and the horizon. The angle and the time of day it was measured can be used to determine a ship's position on a nautical chart.

It's South Georgia Island, Skipper!
Prepare to make landfall, Captain Worsley.
May 10
We finally made it, Skipper!
Nick, this is a splendid moment! Let's get ashore.

There's just one problem, Skipper. The whaling station is on the east coast. We've landed on the west.
We can't sail there, Nick. The *James Caird* is too damaged.

Then we'll do it on foot. The men on Elephant Island are counting on us!
I like your spirit, Nick! We'll rest up for a few days and get back our strength. Then we'll head for the whaling station.

FLUX FACT

After spotting South Georgia Island, a sudden storm gathered and battered the *James Caird*. The crew battled the storm for 9 hours, until it finally passed. "I think most of us had a feeling that the end was very near," wrote Shackleton.

We'll slide down on our coiled rope!
Whoaaaa!
Hold tight, Nick!
We made it!
I'm exhausted. I've got to get some sleep.
No. We'll rest for five minutes and then continue on. If we spend the night here, we'll die from this cold while we sleep.
May 20, 7:00 a.m.
We've got about 12 miles of rough terrain to cross, Skipper.
TWEEEET
We can make it. I know we can.
What? A whistle! It must be the whalers' morning wake-up call! Let's go!

The sound came from the bay! This way!
I-I can't keep up ....
Come on, Nick! Don't give up! We're almost at the whaling station!
You go ahead. I'll catch up to you later.
No, we won't leave you behind. Take my hand.
May 20, 3:00 p.m.
There it is—Stromness Whaling Station!
We marched 36 hours without rest. Come on, let's go in.
I can't move another inch ...
Come on, Nick. Salvation is just ahead.
I-I'm right behind you, Skipper.
Wait for—
Whooaaa!
FZZZZZT!

CHAPTER FIVE
A HAIR-RAISING ADVENTURE
The present
Are you alright down there, Nick? You're missing all the fun!
What?! I can't return now!
I-I'm okay, Dad. I'll be up in second.
I need to look up what happened to Shackleton and his crew!
OOGLE
Reaching the whaling station wasn't the end of the story. The next day, Shackleton rode a ship to rescue the men left on the other side of South Georgia Island.
The rescue from Elephant Island would be much more difficult.
Shackleton tried three times to rescue his crew on Elephant Island. Each time, the ship he sailed became trapped in pack ice and had to return to its port.
Months passed. Shackleton had no way of knowing if his men were still alive.

Finally, on August 30, 1916, Shackleton steamed into the waters off Elephant Island in the *Yelcho*, a rescue ship provided by the government of Chile.
The crew's two-year ordeal was finally over.

Shackleton and his men suffered terrible conditions and difficult obstacles.
But they never gave up hope. They conquered everything they faced.

For that reason, after more than 100 years, we still remember their amazing heroism on an unforgettable voyage.
Now how am I going to explain this shaggy hair?

FLUX FILES

THE SHIP

The *Endurance* was built in Norway in 1912 and was originally named *Polaris*. The vessel was intended to be used for tourists to hunt polar bears. It measured 144 feet (44 m) long and 25 feet (7.6 m) wide. After Sir Ernest Shackleton bought the ship, he renamed it *Endurance*, after his family's motto, "By endurance we conquer." The vessel was equipped with three lifeboats: the *James Caird*, the largest; the *Dudley Docker*, and the *Stancomb Wills*, the smallest.

SHACKLETON'S JOURNEYS

Sir Ernest Shackleton's 1914 expedition was his third to Antarctica. He had tried in 1907 and 1909 to reach the South Pole but had failed in each attempt. In 1909, however, he got within 112 miles (180 km) of the South Pole—the closest anyone in history had reached up to that time. For his accomplishment Shackleton was knighted by British King Edward VII.

OTHER EXPLORERS

Despite his persistent attempts Shackleton was beaten to the South Pole by two explorers. In December 1911 Roald Amundsen of Norway became the first person to reach the bottom of the Earth. Weeks later, in January 1912, Englishman Robert Falcon Scott successfully reached the South Pole. On their return voyage Scott and his four fellow explorers died from starvation and extreme cold.

FINAL VOYAGE

The *Endurance* expedition made Shackleton a hero in England. Eager to continue his explorations, he began a new voyage to Antarctica in 1921 aboard the ship *Quest*. Many of the *Endurance* crewmembers signed on to join their former skipper. The *Quest* arrived at South Georgia Island on January 4, 1922. The next morning, Shackleton, who earlier had been diagnosed with a heart condition, suffered a fatal heart attack. He was 42 years old.

CAPTAIN WORSLEY

After the *Endurance* expedition Captain Frank Worsley joined the British Royal Navy Reserve (RNR). During World War I (1914-1918) he commanded a ship that sunk a German submarine, a deed for which he was awarded the Distinguished Service Order. Over the years Worsley kept in contact with Shackleton. In 1921 he joined his former boss as the captain of the *Quest*, the ship used in Shackleton's ill-fated final expedition.

MAP OF THE *ENDURANCE* EXPEDITION

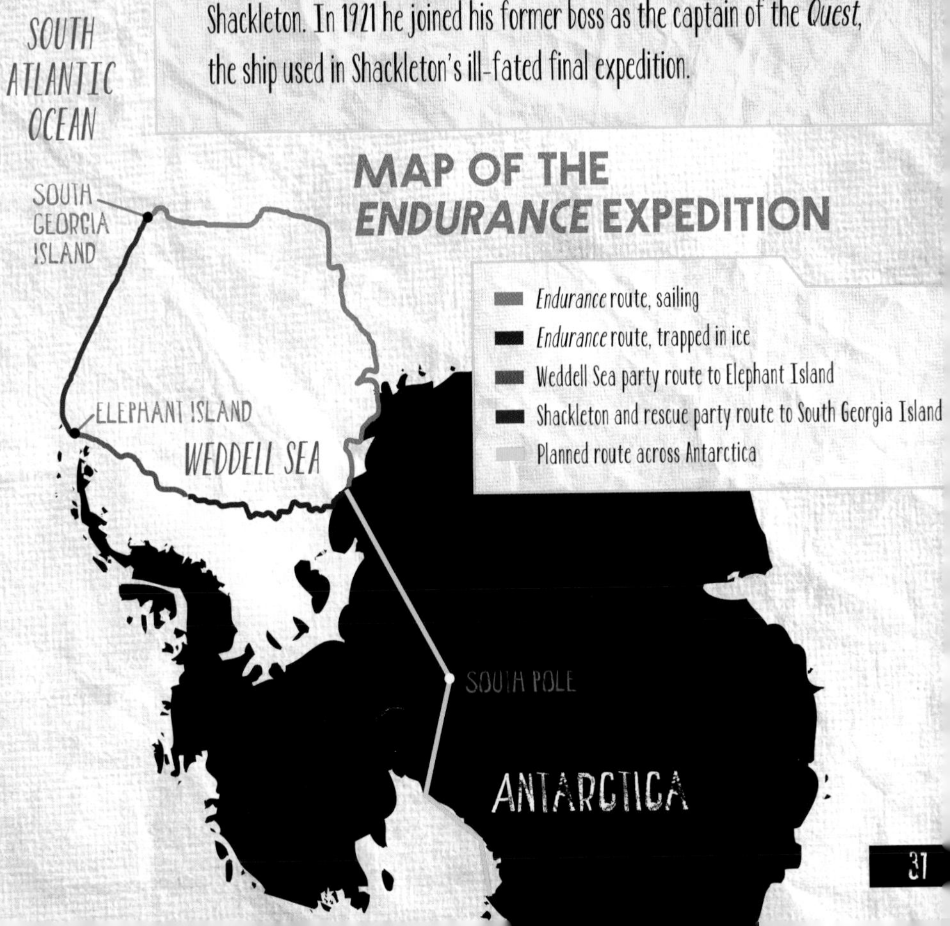

GLOSSARY

EXPEDITION (ek-spuh-DI-shuhn)—a journey with a goal, such as exploring or searching for something

FLOE (FLOH)—a large sheet of floating ice

ISOLATION (eye-suh-LAY-shun)—the condition of being alone

LANDFALL (LAND-fawl)—the act of arriving on land after being on a boat

LIST (LIST)—to lean to one side

ORDEAL (or-DEEL)—a painful or terrible experience

QUEASY (KWEE-zee)—to be sick to one's stomach, or nauseated

SALVAGE (SAL-vij)—to rescue property from a shipwreck, fire, or other disaster

SALVATION (sal-VAY-shuhn)—something or someone that saves or protects

SCARCE (SKAIRSS)—hard to get or find, or available in quantities too small to meet the demand

READ MORE

BRASCH, NICOLAS. *Ernest Shackleton's Antarctic Expedition.* Sensational True Stories. New York: PowerKids Press, 2013.

HANEL, RACHAEL. *Can You Survive Antarctica?* You Choose: Survival. Mankato, Minn.: Capstone Press, 2012.

JOHNSON, KRISTIN. *The Endurance Expedition.* Essential Events. Edina, Minn.: ABDO Pub. Co., 2011.

INTERNET SITES

FactHound offers a safe, fun way to find Internet sites related to this book. All sites on FactHound have been researched by our staff.

Here's all you do:

Visit *www.facthound.com*

Type in this code: 9781491420690

Check out projects, games and lots more at
www.capstonekids.com

ABOUT THE AUTHOR

Nel Yomtov is a writer of children's nonfiction books and graphic novels. He specializes in writing about history, country studies, science, and biography. Nel has written frequently for Capstone, including other Nickolas Flux adventures such as *Peril in Pompeii!: Nickolas Flux and the Eruption of Mount Vesuvius*; *Titanic Disaster!: Nickolas Flux and The Sinking of the Great Ship*; and *Tracking an Assassin!: Nickolas Flux and the Assassination of Abraham Lincoln*. Nel lives in the New York City area.

ALL THE NICKOLAS FLUX ADVENTURES

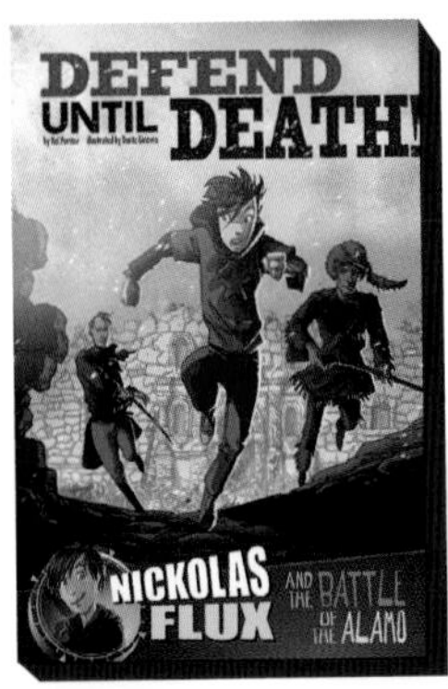